Revolutionary Love: The Biblical Path to Transformation

Dr. Johnnie David Taylor, Jr.

Dr. Johnnie David Taylor, Jr.

Independently published

ISBN: 9798320542850

DEDICATION

To all who journey through the valleys and peaks of life's intricate tapestry, seeking the Divine Light amidst the shadows. This book is dedicated to you, the seekers of truth, the bearers of God's luminous love, and the heralds of grace. May the words within these pages guide you closer to the heart of God, inspiring you to embrace and extend His revolutionary love—a love that transforms, unites, and ushers in a new era of peace and togetherness.

To the One who is Love incarnate, whose boundless and unfailing love reaches into the depths of our being, this work is humbly offered. It is a testament to God's unwavering love, a force potent enough to change the world, one heart at a time. May we all draw nearer to the source of all true love, allowing Him to fill us, transform us, and flow through us, as we become active participants in Love's redemptive work in our world.

CONTENTS

ACKNOWLEDGMENTS

In crafting this book, one beacon of Revolutionary Love has illuminated every page—my mother, Mary Frances Taylor-Park. Her life, a testament to the boundless power of love, has not only shaped my understanding but has also shown the world how true love can transform, heal, and unite. Her compassion, strength, and unwavering faith have taught me that love is not a mere sentiment; it is an active, relentless force that challenges injustice and fosters peace.

This work, while a tribute to Revolutionary Love, is foremost a homage to you, my mother. Your spirit of selfless love and dedication infuses every word, making this book a reflection of the extraordinary love you embody. Thank you, Mother, for being the heart and soul of this journey, my greatest inspiration, and the very definition of love in action.

1 THE BIBLICAL CONCEPT OF LOVE

In the tapestry of human emotions and moral principles, love holds a place of unparalleled importance within the Bible. This divine narrative, sprawling across generations and cultures, places love not merely as a sentiment but as the very essence of God's nature and, consequently, the cornerstone of Christian living. The scriptures, particularly vivid in the teachings of Jesus and the writings of the apostles, elevate love from human affection to a divine mandate, a revolutionary call to transform individuals and societies.

The biblical concept of love, articulated through the ancient texts of the Old and New

Testaments, transcends the often transient and conditional forms of love familiar to human experience. It introduces a love that is selfless, sacrificial, and unconditional—termed agape in the Greek language of the New Testament. This is a love that does not seek its own benefit but pours itself out for the good of others, a love that loves not because the other is lovable but because love is its very nature.

Love as the Foundation of Christian Doctrine

At the core of Christian doctrine is the proclamation that "God is love" (1 John 4:8), a statement that radically defines the nature of God and sets the standard for human interaction. This foundational element is not a passive attribute of God but an active force that brought the world into being, sustains it, and seeks its redemption. The divine love displayed in the creation narrative, the covenants with Abraham and Moses, the poetic yearnings of the Psalms, and the wisdom literature, finds its fullest expression in the person of Jesus Christ.

Christ's teachings, as recorded in the Gospels, reiterate and expand upon the Old Testament commandments to love God and neighbor. Yet, He goes further, challenging His followers to love their enemies, lend without expecting anything in return, and do good to those who hate them (Luke 6:27-35). Through His life, death, and resurrection, Jesus exemplifies this love, breaking down barriers of sin and separation, offering forgiveness and reconciliation, and calling all to a life of loving service.

The apostolic writings further emphasize love as the hallmark of the Christian community. Paul's letters, particularly, are rich with instructions to live out love in practical, everyday actions, underscoring that love is the fulfillment of the law (Romans 13:10) and the greatest of all virtues (1 Corinthians 13:13). The epistles of John echo this theme, reminding believers that love is both an evidence of God's presence in their lives and a commandment to be obeyed.

Love's Transformative Power

The revolutionary power of biblical love lies in its ability to transform. First, it transforms the individual, inviting them into a relationship with God characterized by love and leading to a life changed from the inside out. As believers grow in understanding and living out this love, they find their attitudes, priorities, and actions increasingly aligned with God's will. This personal transformation is the first step in a wider societal change.

Second, love transforms relationships. By commanding His followers to love not only their neighbors but also their enemies, Jesus sets forth a radical new way of relating to others. This love seeks reconciliation, practices forgiveness, and extends grace, breaking cycles of retaliation and violence and building communities of peace and mutual support.

Finally, love has the power to transform societies. When individuals and communities live out the biblical mandate to love, they challenge the prevailing social norms of power, greed, and self-interest. They become agents of change, advocating for justice, caring for the poor and marginalized, and working towards a world that reflects God's kingdom, where love reigns supreme.

A Call to Revolutionary Love

"Revolutionary Love: The Biblical Path to Transformation" invites readers on a journey to rediscover the radical, transformative power of biblical love. It challenges the modern conceptions of love, calling for a return to the selfless, sacrificial love exemplified by Jesus—a love that dares to change the world, one act of kindness at a time.

This book aims not only to explore the biblical teachings on love but also to inspire readers to live out these teachings in their daily lives. By doing so, it envisions a community of believers who embody God's love, bearing witness to its power to heal, restore, and transform.

As we embark on this journey together, let us open our hearts to the revolutionary call of love, allowing it to transform us and, through us, the world around us. In a world marked by division and despair, let us be bearers of hope, practitioners of grace, and agents of God's unending love.

2 LOVE FOR ENEMIES

In the heart of the Sermon on the Mount, Jesus presents teachings that invert the expected norms of social conduct, none more revolutionary than the command to love one's enemies. This chapter delves into the teachings found in Matthew 5:43-44 and Luke 6:27, 35, exploring the radical nature of this love and its implications for both personal growth and communal harmony.

The Command to Love One's Enemies

"Ye have heard that it hath been said, Thou shalt love thy neighbour, and hate thine enemy. But I say unto you, Love your enemies, bless them that curse you, do good to them that hate you, and pray for them which despitefully use you, and persecute you;" (Matthew 5:43-44, KJV). Similarly, Luke 6:27, 35 reiterates, "But I say unto you which hear, Love your enemies, do good to them which hate you... But love ye your enemies, and do good, and lend, hoping for nothing again; and your reward shall be great, and ye shall be the children of the Highest: for he is kind unto the unthankful and to the evil."

These passages reflect Jesus' call to a higher standard of love, one that transcends natural inclinations and societal expectations. It's a directive that doesn't merely suggest tolerance or passive acceptance but active, intentional love towards those who oppose, harm, or persecute. This love is neither emotional affection nor based on the worthiness of the recipient but is a reflection of God's unconditional love for all.

The Radical Nature of Loving One's Enemies

The concept of loving one's enemies is as counterintuitive today as it was two millennia ago. In a world where retribution and self-defense are often justified reactions to aggression, the call to love, bless, and pray for one's adversaries is revolutionary. It challenges the very core of human nature, which seeks justice as recompense and protection from harm.

This radical love is predicated on the recognition of the inherent worth of every individual, created in the image of God, and the understanding that God's love is universal, extending even to those who reject or oppose Him. It's a love that seeks reconciliation over victory, understanding over judgment, and healing over punishment.

The Transformation through Loving One's Enemies

Loving one's enemies has profound transformative potential for the individual. It liberates from the cycle of anger, bitterness, and desire for vengeance that can consume one's heart and mind. It fosters inner peace, joy, and a sense of freedom, as one obeys God's command and trusts Him with the outcome. Practicing this love cultivates virtues such as patience, kindness, and self-control, molding the believer more into the likeness of Christ.

Moreover, this love can lead to the transformation of the enemy. Encounters with unconditional love and forgiveness can soften hearts, dismantle prejudices, and open doors for dialogue and reconciliation. It bears witness to the power of God's love, potentially leading others to seek and experience His transformative grace.

Practical Implications for Personal and Communal Life

The command to love one's enemies has far-reaching implications for both personal behavior and community dynamics. Individually, it calls for self-examination and the deliberate choice to respond with love in situations of conflict. It means praying for those who oppose or harm us, seeking their good, and being open to the possibility of reconciliation. It requires reliance on God's strength and wisdom, as loving enemies is not achievable through human effort alone.

Communally, this love can radically alter the landscape of relationships within families, churches, and societies. It promotes a culture of forgiveness, peace, and mutual respect, countering the narratives of division and hostility. In conflicts ranging from interpersonal disputes to societal or international tensions, the biblical command to love enemies offers a pathway to healing and unity.

Churches and Christian communities can model this love through their outreach and ministry, extending grace and assistance without discrimination. They can facilitate dialogues, participate in peacemaking efforts, and support those affected by conflict, demonstrating the love of Christ in tangible ways.

Living out Revolutionary Love

To live out this revolutionary love, believers are encouraged to cultivate a personal relationship with God, allowing His love to fill and transform their hearts. Engaging in regular prayer, including intercession for enemies, studying the scriptures, and participating in communal worship and fellowship, strengthens one's faith and capacity to love as God loves.

Practical steps may include reaching out to those from whom we are estranged, offering forgiveness to those who have wronged us, or serving those who oppose us without expecting anything in return. It involves advocating for justice and peace, standing in solidarity with the oppressed, and working towards reconciliation in divided communities.

Conclusion

The biblical command to love one's enemies stands as one of the most challenging and transformative teachings of Jesus. It calls believers to a radical love that has the power to change hearts, mend broken relationships, and heal divided communities. This love is not a mere ideal but a practical, actionable mandate that requires daily commitment and reliance on God's grace. As we embody this revolutionary love, we bear witness to the kingdom of God, where love reigns supreme and enemies become friends.

.

3 THE DANGER OF MISPLACED LOVE

In the journey of faith, the allure of the world often presents a formidable challenge, pulling the believer's heart away from the divine path designed by God. This chapter delves into the teachings of Jesus and the apostles regarding the perils of misplaced love—specifically, the love for material wealth and the broader category of worldly desires. Through an examination of Matthew 6:24, Luke 16:13, and 1 John 2:15, we uncover the inherent conflict between the love for God and the love for worldly things, aiming to illuminate the idolatries that can ensnare the heart.

The Conflict between Love for God and Love for Worldly Things

"No man can serve two masters: for either he will hate the one, and love the other; or else he will hold to the one, and despise the other. Ye cannot serve God and mammon." (Matthew 6:24, KJV). Echoed in Luke 16:13, this declaration by Jesus highlights a fundamental truth about human devotion: it is impossible to equally commit to conflicting priorities. The term "mammon," Aramaic in origin, encompasses wealth, riches, and material possessions, symbolizing the broader concept of worldly desires that can dominate one's life.

Similarly, the apostle John admonishes, "Love not the world, neither the things that are in the world. If any man love the world, the love of the Father is not in him." (1 John 2:15, KJV). These scriptures collectively emphasize a stark warning: a heart captivated by the allure of worldly pleasures and possessions is a heart drifting away from God. This misplaced love not only jeopardizes one's relationship with the Creator but also ensnares the believer in a cycle of temporary satisfaction and enduring emptiness.

Identifying Idolatries of the Heart

The human heart is a battleground of affections, where desires for security, significance, and satisfaction vie for supremacy. When the love for God is supplanted by a love for the world, it signals the presence of idolatry—attributing ultimate value to something other than God. This idolatry may manifest in various forms: an insatiable pursuit of wealth, an obsession with status or power, a preoccupation with physical beauty, or an unyielding quest for pleasure.

These idols of the heart are not always conspicuous; they often masquerade as commendable ambitions, legitimate needs, or harmless indulgences. Yet, their danger lies in their ability to dethrone God in one's life, redirecting worship, trust, and love away from Him and towards transient, created things. This displacement not only diminishes one's capacity to love God wholeheartedly but also impedes the fulfillment of the command to love one's neighbor, as resources, time, and energy are consumed by self-serving pursuits.

Addressing Idolatries of the Heart

Confronting and overcoming the idolatries of the heart requires a deliberate, multifaceted approach grounded in the transformative power of the Gospel. The first step involves recognition and repentance—a humble acknowledgment of one's susceptibility to worldly allurements and a sincere turning away from them. This repentance is not a mere emotional response but a decisive shift in allegiance, from serving the idols of the heart to serving God alone.

The renewing of the mind through engagement with Scripture plays a pivotal role in this process. The truths of God's Word counteract the lies propagated by the world, revealing the fleeting nature of worldly pleasures and the enduring satisfaction found in God. As believers meditate on and internalize these truths, their affections are realigned, and their values reshaped.

Fostering a deep, intimate relationship with God is essential to displacing the idols of the heart. Through prayer, worship, and communion with God, believers experience the depth of His love, the richness of His grace, and the sufficiency of His provision. This divine encounter cultivates a love for God that supersedes all others, transforming the heart's desires and priorities.

Community accountability and support are invaluable in this journey. The Christian community offers encouragement, wisdom, and correction, helping believers to navigate the challenges of living counter to the culture in a world that glorifies materialism and self-indulgence. Through fellowship, discipleship, and mutual edification, believers are strengthened to resist the temptations of the world and to pursue God with undivided hearts.

The Transformation through Rightly Placed Love

The transition from misplaced love to rightly placed love is marked by profound transformation. As believers prioritize their love for God and align their desires with His will, they find true contentment, peace, and joy that the world cannot offer. This transformation impacts not only their personal lives but also their relationships and communities, as they become conduits of God's love, grace, and generosity.

Rightly placed love manifests in a life characterized by generosity, service, and compassion. Freed from the grip of materialism and selfish ambitions, believers are empowered to love their neighbors selflessly, to give generously of their resources, and to invest in eternal treasures. This lifestyle bears witness to the transformative power of the Gospel, challenging the values of the world and inviting others to discover the incomparable love of God.

Conclusion

The dangers of misplaced love are stark, yet the

promise of transformation through rightly placed love is profound. By recognizing and addressing the idolatries of the heart, believers embark on a journey of continual renewal, where love for God and love for others becomes the defining mark of their lives. This chapter calls for a radical reevaluation of priorities and affections, urging believers to forsake the fleeting pleasures of the world for the surpassing worth of knowing and loving God. In doing so, they step into their true identity as children of the Most High, agents of revolutionary love in a world desperately in need of transformation.

4 LOVE AS A FULFILLMENT OF THE LAW

In the mosaic of biblical teachings, love not only serves as the pinnacle expression of divine character but also as the principle that fulfills and transcends the law given to Moses. This chapter explores the profound relationship between love and the law, particularly through the lens of Romans 13:8-10 and Galatians 5:14, highlighting how love both upholds and elevates the moral and ethical standards set forth in the Old Testament.

The Interconnection of Love and the Law

"Owe no man any thing, but to love one another: for he that loveth another hath fulfilled the law." (Romans 13:8, KJV). Paul's epistle to the Romans encapsulates a revolutionary concept: the entirety of the law is fulfilled in the single act of loving one's neighbor. This assertion is not a dismissal of the law but an acknowledgment of love's capacity to meet and exceed the law's demands. Love, in its purest form, instinctively avoids actions that harm others, thereby adhering to the law's intent without being constrained by its letter.

Galatians 5:14 reiterates this theme, "For all the law is fulfilled in one word, even in this; Thou shalt love thy neighbour as thyself." Here, Paul distills the essence of the law into a directive that is both simple and profound. Love becomes the lens through which the believer views and interacts with the world, transforming adherence to the law from a duty to a natural expression of faith.

Upholding the Law through Love

The Old Testament law, with its detailed commandments and statutes, provided a framework for the Israelites to live in a manner pleasing to God, regulating aspects of social justice, personal morality, and religious observance. While the law delineated what was required of God's people, it was not an end in itself. Its ultimate purpose was to guide them toward a life characterized by holiness, justice, and love.

In the New Testament, Jesus and the apostles reveal that the fulfillment of the law is not found in rigid adherence to its commands but in the embodiment of love. Love naturally upholds the law by seeking the good of the other, thereby avoiding actions that would contravene God's commandments. When love guides the believer's actions, there is no need for an external checklist, for love does no harm to a neighbor (Romans 13:10).

Transcending the Law through Love

While love upholds the law, it also transcends it. Love goes beyond the minimum requirements of the law, calling for a proactive pursuit of the well-being of others. It challenges believers to not only refrain from doing harm but to actively do good, to not only love those who are lovable but to love the unlovable, and to extend grace and forgiveness even to those who do not "deserve" it. This is the love that Jesus demonstrated and commanded His followers to emulate—a love

that sacrifices, serves, and seeks reconciliation.
The transformative power of this love is evident in the ethical living it engenders. A life governed by love reflects the character of God, bears witness to the truth of the Gospel, and impacts the world. It elevates the discourse on ethics from mere compliance with moral laws to the cultivation of virtues that mirror divine love. It challenges societal norms and values, advocating for justice, compassion, and humility in a world often ruled by selfishness and greed.

Practical Implications for Ethical Living

The implications of viewing love as the fulfillment of the law are vast, affecting every aspect of personal and communal life. It calls for an introspection of one's motivations, attitudes, and actions, aligning them with the principle of love. It encourages believers to consider not only what is lawful but what is beneficial and edifying for others (1 Corinthians 10:23).

In practical terms, this love manifests in forgiveness extended to those who have wronged us, generosity toward those in need, advocacy for the marginalized and oppressed, and kindness and patience in our interactions with others. It means choosing service over self-interest, unity over division, and peace over conflict.

The Transformative Power of Love

The law, with its commandments and ordinances, was a tutor leading to Christ (Galatians 3:24), in whom the fullness of God's love was revealed. In Christ, believers are called to a higher standard of living, where love is both the motivation and the goal. This love has the power to transform hearts and minds, to renew relationships, and to impact society positively.

As the believer's heart becomes attuned to the love of God, ethical decisions are no longer driven by obligation but by a genuine desire to reflect God's love in the world. This transformation is the work of the Holy Spirit, who enables believers to live out the commandment of love, fulfilling the law in ways that mere human effort never could.

Conclusion

In the biblical narrative, love emerges as the

supreme ethic, the principle that both fulfills and transcends the law given through Moses. It calls believers to a life marked by actions and attitudes that reflect God's love, challenging them to look beyond the letter of the law to its spirit. As this chapter has explored, love's transformative power not only upholds the ethical standards of the law but elevates them, guiding believers toward a way of living that honors God and serves others. In "Revolutionary Love: The Biblical Path to Transformation," the journey into understanding and embodying this love continues, promising a path of personal growth and societal change.

5 LOVE'S EXPRESSIONS AND ACTIONS

In the quest to understand the depth and breadth of biblical love, two passages stand as pillars illuminating its essence: 1 Corinthians 13, known as the love chapter, and 1 John 3:16-18, which ties love to tangible acts of compassion. This chapter explores the characteristics and behaviors of biblical love as delineated in these scriptures, and its pivotal role in community building and reconciliation.

The Essence of Biblical Love

1 Corinthians 13 offers a sublime portrait of love, elevating it above all spiritual gifts and accomplishments. "Though I speak with the tongues of men and of angels, and have not

charity (love), I am become as sounding brass, or a tinkling cymbal." (1 Corinthians 13:1, KJV). Love is depicted not as an emotion but as a principle guiding all actions. It's patient and kind; it does not envy or boast, is not proud, rude, self-seeking, or easily angered; it keeps no record of wrongs. Love rejoices in truth, always protects, trusts, hopes, perseveres, and never fails.

These characteristics form a blueprint for living in accordance with God's will, challenging believers to embody love in all interactions. This love is agape—selfless, sacrificial, unconditional—reflecting God's own love for humanity. It calls for a love that extends beyond feelings to actions, a love that is lived out daily in relationships with others.

Love in Action: The Model of Christ

1 John 3:16-18 further emphasizes the action-oriented nature of love, pointing to Jesus as the exemplar: "Hereby perceive we the love of God, because he laid down his life for us: and we ought to lay down our lives for the brethren. But whoso hath this world's good, and seeth his brother have need, and shutteth up his bowels of compassion from him, how

dwelleth the love of God in him? My little children, let us not love in word, neither in tongue; but in deed and in truth." (KJV).

This passage underscores that love is demonstrated through sacrifice and practical care for others. It suggests that the true measure of love is not in declarations or feelings but in willingness to act on behalf of others' well-being, even to the point of personal sacrifice. This sets a high standard for believers, calling them to mirror Christ's love in their lives by being attentive to the needs of others and responding with compassion and generosity.

Love's Role in Community Building

Biblical love serves as a cornerstone for community building, fostering relationships marked by mutual respect, understanding, and care. In a community governed by such love, differences are bridged, and unity is fostered. This love compels believers to look beyond personal interests to the common good, promoting peace, harmony, and collective flourishing.

Moreover, love motivates believers to bear one another's burdens, celebrate each other's successes, and support each other in times of need. It encourages forgiveness, reconciliation, and a commitment to each other's spiritual and personal growth. In essence, love becomes the adhesive that binds the community together, reflecting the kingdom of God on earth.

Love's Role in Reconciliation

The biblical mandate to love also plays a crucial role in reconciliation, both within the community of believers and in the broader society. Love drives the pursuit of justice, urging believers to address issues of inequality, oppression, and conflict. It calls for honest conversations, a willingness to listen and understand, and a commitment to making amends and restoring relationships.

In scenarios of conflict, love acts as a mediator, guiding parties toward empathy, forgiveness, and peace. It challenges the natural inclination towards retaliation with the divine call to bless those who curse us and do good to those who harm us. By choosing love, believers pave the way for healing and reconciliation, demonstrating the power of God's love to transform hearts and mend brokenness.

The Transformative Power of Love in Action

The narrative of love in 1 Corinthians 13 and 1 John 3:16-18 culminates in a powerful truth: love, when genuinely practiced, has the capacity to transform individuals and communities. It molds believers into the likeness of Christ, enabling them to live out their faith in ways that draw others to God. Love in action challenges societal norms, advocating for a kingdom where love reigns supreme, and every person is valued and cared for.

The call to love is, therefore, not just a moral or ethical directive but a way of life that embodies the very essence of the Gospel. It demands courage, humility, and perseverance, promising, in return, a life marked by deep satisfaction, joy, and purpose. As believers commit to loving in deed and in truth, they bear witness to the revolutionary love of God—a love that heals, unites, and transforms.

Conclusion

In summary, love, as outlined in 1 Corinthians 13 and 1 John 3:16-18, is the hallmark of the

Christian faith, a radical principle that calls for action beyond words. It is the foundation upon which communities of faith are built and the catalyst for reconciliation and healing. This chapter has explored the multifaceted expressions and transformative power of biblical love, inviting believers to embrace this love as a way of life. As we journey through "Revolutionary Love: The Biblical Path to Transformation," may we be inspired to live out this love, making it visible in our actions and interactions, and thus participating in the transformation of our world.

6 THE LOVE OF GOD FOR HUMANITY

In the grand narrative of the Bible, the love of God for humanity stands as the central theme, a divine thread weaving through creation, fall, redemption, and restoration. This chapter delves into the profound demonstrations of God's love, particularly through the lens of John 3:16, Romans 5:8, and 1 John 4:9-10, to explore the depth of divine affection for mankind and its implications for human identity and purpose.

The Ultimate Demonstration of Divine Love

"For God so loved the world, that he gave his only begotten Son, that whosoever believeth in him should not perish, but have everlasting life." (John 3:16, KJV). This verse encapsulates the essence of the Gospel—the sacrificial love of God that propelled Him to offer His only Son, Jesus Christ, for the salvation of humanity. It speaks of a love that transcends human understanding, a love that chooses to redeem rather than condemn, to give life rather than exact death.

Similarly, Romans 5:8 declares, "But God commendeth his love toward us, in that, while we were yet sinners, Christ died for us." The apostle Paul emphasizes that the demonstration of God's love was not conditional upon human righteousness or merit; rather, it was displayed in the midst of human rebellion and sin. This act of love provides a radical redefinition of love, marked by grace, mercy, and forgiveness.

1 John 4:9-10 further illuminates the nature of this love: "In this was manifested the love of God toward us, because that God sent his only begotten Son into the world, that we might live through him. Herein is love, not that we loved God, but that he loved us, and sent his Son to be the propitiation for our sins." These verses highlight that divine love is initiatory and

sacrificial, aimed at restoring the broken relationship between God and humanity.

Implications of Divine Love for Human Identity

The love of God for humanity is not just a theological concept; it has profound implications for human identity. Understanding that one is deeply loved by God imparts a sense of worth and value that is independent of achievements, status, or recognition. This divine love affirms that each person is created in the image of God, designed for relationship with Him, and endowed with inherent dignity and purpose.

Moreover, the realization of God's love invites individuals into a journey of transformation. As believers grasp the depth of God's love for them, reflected in the sacrifice of Christ, they are motivated to respond in love, surrender, and obedience. This understanding of being loved by God becomes the foundation for a new identity—as children of God, heirs of His kingdom, and ambassadors of His love in the world.

The Purpose Defined by Divine Love

God's love not only bestows identity but also imparts purpose. The knowledge of being loved by God and saved through Christ propels believers to live lives that reflect this love to others. It calls them to love God in return and to extend His love to their neighbors, embodying the commandments that Jesus described as the greatest (Matthew 22:37-39).

This divine love also inspires a commitment to justice, mercy, and humility, as outlined in Micah 6:8. It motivates believers to act as agents of reconciliation, peace, and healing in a broken world. The purpose defined by divine love encompasses both personal sanctification—growing into the likeness of Christ—and participation in God's redemptive mission for humanity and creation.

Moreover, understanding the sacrificial nature of God's love challenges believers to consider their own lives as offerings poured out in service to God and others. It reframes perspectives on suffering, sacrifice, and service, inviting believers to find joy and fulfillment in participating in Christ's sufferings and in sharing the hope found in His resurrection.

Conclusion

The love of God for humanity, as demonstrated through the gift of Jesus Christ, stands as the most profound revelation of divine character and the cornerstone of Christian faith. This chapter has explored the depth and implications of this love, highlighting its transformative power in defining human identity and purpose.

As we continue to journey through "Revolutionary Love: The Biblical Path to Transformation," may the knowledge of God's immense love for us shape our understanding of who we are and why we are here. May it compel us to live lives marked by love, service, and sacrifice, reflecting the image of our Creator and advancing His kingdom on earth. In grasping the width, length, height, and depth of God's love, we find not only the essence of our being but also the path to true fulfillment and joy.

7 RESPONDING TO GOD'S LOVE

The journey of faith is, at its core, a response to the unfathomable love of God—a love so profound and revolutionary that it beckons a reciprocal expression of love towards God and a selfless love towards others. This chapter draws upon John 14:15, 21, 23-24, and 1 John 4:19-21 to explore the dynamics of responding to God's love, highlighting the call to love God and others, as well as navigating the challenges and embracing the joys that come with living in accordance with this divine love.

The Call to Love God and Others

In John 14:15, Jesus articulates a simple yet profound criterion for expressing love towards Him: "If ye love me, keep my commandments." This directive is further expanded in verses 21, 23-24, where Jesus links love for Him with obedience to His teachings, promising the indwelling presence of the Father and Himself as a reward for such love and obedience. Love for God, therefore, is not a mere sentiment but is demonstrated through a life lived in adherence to His commandments—a life that mirrors Jesus' own love, obedience, and submission to the Father's will.

1 John 4:19-21 encapsulates the essence of responding to God's love, stating, "We love him, because he first loved us." The apostle John underscores that our capacity to love is fundamentally a response to experiencing God's love. This love is not to remain inward-focused but is to be extended outward in love for our brothers and sisters: "If a man say, I love God, and hateth his brother, he is a liar... And this commandment have we from him, That he who loveth God love his brother also."

The Manifestation of Love in Obedience

Responding to God's love involves more than emotional affection; it necessitates a transformation in how we live. Obedience to

God's commandments is the tangible manifestation of our love for Him—a love that prioritizes His will above our desires, seeks to glorify Him in all aspects of our lives, and aligns our actions with His character and teachings. This obedience is not burdensome but is borne out of gratitude and a deep sense of connection with God, facilitated by the Holy Spirit.

Loving others as a reflection of God's love is perhaps one of the most concrete expressions of our love for God. It challenges us to look beyond our prejudices, to forgive as we have been forgiven, to serve without expectation of reward, and to extend grace and kindness even when it's underserved. This outward expression of love validates our profession of love for God, making our faith visible and impactful in the world around us.

Navigating the Challenges

Living in response to God's love is not without its challenges. In a world that often values self-interest, power, and material wealth, choosing a path of love and obedience to God can be countercultural and, at times, difficult. Persecution, misunderstanding, and rejection may come from outside the faith community, and sometimes, disappointingly, from within.

Moreover, the call to love others can be complicated by personal conflicts, deep-seated resentments, and the messiness of human relationships. Forgiving those who have hurt us, loving those who oppose us, and serving those who may not appreciate our efforts can stretch our capacity to love.

However, these challenges also serve as opportunities for growth. They refine our faith, deepen our reliance on God, and sharpen our understanding of what it means to love as Christ loves. The journey involves a continual process of surrendering our will to God's, allowing His love to heal, restore, and transform us.

Embracing the Joys

The response to God's love, while challenging, is also a source of profound joy and fulfillment. There is a deep peace that comes from living in alignment with God's will, a sense of purpose gleaned from serving others, and a joy in witnessing the transformative impact of God's love in the lives of those around us.

Furthermore, the act of loving others creates a ripple effect, fostering a sense of community, belonging, and mutual care that reflects the kingdom of God on earth. The experience of God's presence, the assurance of His love, and the hope of eternal life with Him are incomparable treasures that sustain believers in their journey.

Conclusion

Responding to God's love by loving Him and others is the essence of the Christian walk—a journey marked by obedience, service, and transformation. This chapter has explored the multifaceted aspects of responding to divine love, acknowledging the challenges but also highlighting the indescribable joy that comes from living out this love.

As we progress through "Revolutionary Love: The Biblical Path to Transformation," let us be encouraged to deepen our response to God's love, to pursue obedience with passion, and to love others with the selflessness that reflects the heart of God. In doing so, we not only find our true purpose and fulfillment but also become vessels of God's transformative love in a world in desperate need of His grace.

8 LOVE'S VICTORY AND REWARD

In the tapestry of Christian doctrine, the concept of love not only serves as the golden thread that binds together the teachings of Christ but also as the enduring force that triumphs over adversity. This chapter reflects on Romans 8:35-39 and Revelation 2:19, exploring the invincible nature of love in the face of trials and persecutions, and the sublime promise of eternal life and reward that awaits those who, motivated by love, persevere in their faith.

The Indomitable Nature of Love Amid Adversity

Paul's epistle to the Romans contains one of

the most poignant affirmations of the power of love found in Scripture. In Romans 8:35-39, Paul poses a series of rhetorical questions that challenge anything in creation to separate us from the love of Christ, concluding that nothing can. This passage reassures believers that, despite the tribulations, distress, persecution, famine, nakedness, peril, or sword they may face, the love of Christ remains unshakable. It is a testament to the fact that love—God's love for us and our love for Him—is not weakened by hardships but rather is made manifest through them.

This enduring nature of love amid trials is not merely theoretical but is evidenced in the lives of countless believers who have faced persecution throughout history and into the present day. Their steadfastness in the face of adversity serves as a powerful witness to the world of the transformative and sustaining power of God's love.

Love's Victory in Perseverance

Revelation 2:19 commends the church in Thyatira for their love, faith, service, and patient endurance, noting that their latter works exceed the first. This verse encapsulates the progressive nature of the Christian journey—one that is marked by increasing fidelity, love, and service despite the challenges encountered. The mention of "patient endurance" is particularly significant, highlighting that perseverance in faith and love is not passive but an active, continuous effort that is recognized and commended by Christ Himself.

The victory of love is thus twofold: it is present in the daily triumphs over trials and temptations, and it is ultimately realized in the fulfillment of God's promises. Love's victory is manifested in lives transformed by the Gospel, in relationships restored by forgiveness, and in communities rebuilt on the principles of God's kingdom.

The Promise of Eternal Life and Reward

The culmination of love's victory is the promise of eternal life and reward for those who love God and persevere in faith. Romans 8:35-39 assures us that, in the face of life's greatest challenges, nothing can sever the bond of love that unites us with Christ. This unbreakable connection is the source of our hope and the guarantee of our inheritance—a life eternal with God, free from pain, sorrow, and death.

Moreover, Revelation 2:19 suggests that the faithfulness and growth of the believers in love and service are not overlooked by God but are indeed rewarded. The New Testament is replete with assurances that God rewards those who diligently seek Him (Hebrews 11:6) and that there is laid up a crown of righteousness for all who have loved His appearing (2 Timothy 4:8).

Navigating the Path to Victory and Reward

Embracing love's victory and the promise of eternal reward requires a steadfast commitment to loving God and others, even in the face of adversity. It calls for a reliance on the Holy Spirit to sustain and empower us, a commitment to the Word of God as our guide and comfort, and a community of believers with whom we can share the journey.

The path to victory and reward is marked by daily decisions to choose love over indifference, forgiveness over bitterness, and faith over fear. It involves using our gifts and resources to serve others and to advance God's kingdom, knowing that our labor in the Lord is not in vain (1 Corinthians 15:58).

Conclusion

The narrative of love's victory and reward is central to the Christian faith, offering both comfort and challenge to believers. It reassures us of the invincible nature of God's love for us and the ultimate victory that awaits those who persevere in loving God and others. As we close this chapter on "Revolutionary Love: The Biblical Path to Transformation," let us hold fast to the promise that nothing can separate us from the love of God in Christ Jesus our Lord. May this assurance inspire us to live with courage, to love with abandon, and to press on towards the reward that awaits those faithful in love and deed. In the enduring power of love, we find our strength, our hope, and our ultimate victory.

9 EMBRACING AND EXTENDING REVOLUTIONARY LOVE

As we reach the culmination of our journey through "Revolutionary Love: The Biblical Path to Transformation," we find ourselves standing on the precipice of profound insight and divine invitation. This exploration has illuminated the essence of biblical love—not as mere sentiment, but as the very heartbeat of God's interaction with humanity and the central commandment for those who follow Christ. We have traversed the depths of God's sacrificial love for us, the call to love Him in return, the radical mandate to love our enemies, and the transformative power of love in personal and communal spheres. Now, we are beckoned to respond, to embody this revolutionary love in a world desperate for hope and healing.

The Essence and Importance of Biblical Love

Biblical love, as revealed in the scriptures, is agape: selfless, sacrificial, and unconditional. It is a love that transcends human understanding that chooses to give without expectation of return that sees the image of God in every person. This love was embodied perfectly in Jesus Christ, who, though divine, stooped to serve, and though sinless, chose to die for the redemption of humanity. The essence of biblical love, therefore, is not found in the magnitude of one's feelings but in the depth of one's actions—actions that reflect God's character, prioritize others' welfare, and are guided by truth and justice.

The importance of this love cannot be overstated. In a world fractured by division, strife, and indifference, the radical, counter-cultural love of the Bible offers a blueprint for restoration and unity. It challenges prevailing narratives of self-interest and retaliation with principles of forgiveness, service, and compassion. More than ever, the church and its constituents are called to model this love, demonstrating its power to heal, to unite, and to transform.

A Call to Action for Individuals and Churches

The journey through the concepts and demonstrations of biblical love culminates in a compelling call to action for both individuals and church communities. As individuals, we are urged to internalize this love, allowing it to transform our hearts and minds, and then to externalize it through our interactions with others. This means prioritizing daily acts of kindness, extending forgiveness, advocating for justice, and serving those in need—actions that emanate from a heart attuned to God's love and compassion.

For churches, the call to action is to be beacons of God's love in their communities and beyond. This involves creating inclusive, welcoming spaces where individuals from all walks of life can experience the tangible love of God. It means mobilizing resources to address societal issues, championing causes that promote dignity and respect for all, and engaging in peacemaking efforts that bridge divides. Churches are called to be exemplars of love in action, reflecting the diverse and unified body of Christ to a watching world.

Reflections on the Future Hope for a World Transformed by Love

As we reflect on the future hope for a world transformed by love, we are reminded of the prophetic visions in Scripture that depict a redeemed creation where peace and righteousness dwell. This vision, though yet to be fully realized, is brought closer to fruition each time an individual or community chooses to live out the principles of biblical love. The transformative power of love has the potential to effect change on a global scale, reshaping societies, restoring relationships, and renewing hope.

The future hope for a world transformed by love is not a passive waiting for divine intervention but an active participation in God's redemptive work. It is a future crafted by countless acts of love, both large and small, that collectively bear witness to the kingdom of God. It is a future where love triumphs over hate, unity over division, and grace over judgment.

Conclusion

In closing, "Revolutionary Love: The Biblical Path to Transformation" serves not only as a reflection on the multifaceted aspects of love as depicted in the Bible but also as an invitation to live out this love in a world that yearns for authenticity and healing. As individuals and as church communities, we are called to embody the revolutionary love of God, a love that sacrifices, serves, and seeks the good of others.

May we rise to this call with courage and conviction, allowing God's love to transform us from the inside out, and committing ourselves to be agents of love in a world in need. In doing so, we align ourselves with the redemptive heart of God, participating in the unfolding story of a creation renewed and restored by love. The journey of embodying revolutionary love is both a privilege and a responsibility, a source of joy and a mission of utmost importance. Let us embark on this journey with hope, for in love, we find the true path to transformation and the promise of a future filled with love, peace and joy from God.

ABOUT THE AUTHOR

Dr. Johnnie D. Taylor, Jr. is not just an author; he is a visionary leader whose career spans across military service to key roles in the corporate world. Having served as the Chief Operations Officer and Managing Director, Contracts of a multi-million dollar enterprise, Johnnie has pioneered strategic changes that have sculpted the landscape of business and defense contracting. With a wealth of experience under his belt, he has driven organizations toward excellence with a keen focus on quality-based strategic planning and leadership, yielding unparalleled growth and stakeholder value by underpinning the organizational, customer, and leadership interactions with Radical Love.

His journey from a dedicated United States Air Force Commander to a pivotal figure in federal contracting and business operations showcases a relentless pursuit of excellence. A doctorate in Business Administration in Quality Systems Management and Religious Education combined with a rich foundation in behavioral science, counseling, adult education, and electronic technology, underscores his multifaceted expertise. Johnnie's distinguished career is decorated with high honors, reflecting his commitment to leadership, innovation, and service.

Beyond his professional achievements, Johnnie's work is a testament to his profound understanding of transformation through love, leadership, and community building. A certified John Maxwell Coach and a recognized speaker, he brings insights from his extensive background to inspire and guide individuals and organizations towards achieving their highest potential.

He is currently serves as the National Director of Education for his church affiliation and Pastor. This book promises to be a beacon for anyone seeking to navigate the complexities of personal growth, forgiveness, and the practical application of biblical principles in modern life.

Made in the USA
Middletown, DE
30 March 2024